# Feeling *Festive*

### Eight beautiful cards in on-trend folksy style for all your friends and family this Christmas

**Designed by:** Felicity Hall **Stitch time:** 4–6 hours each

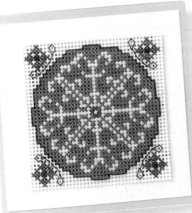

## Materials

- 14 count white perforated paper, 4 ½x4 ½in (11x11cm) piece for each
- Pale green card, 4x8 ¼in (10.5x21cm)
- White card, 3 ¾x3 ¾in (9.5x9.5cm) for each

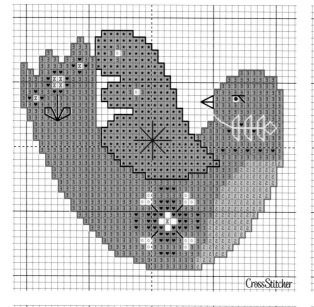

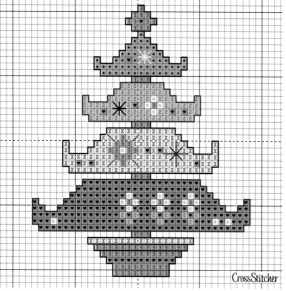

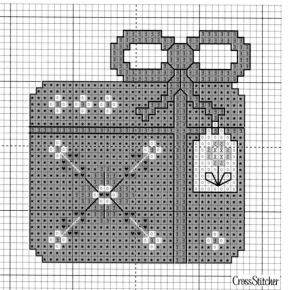

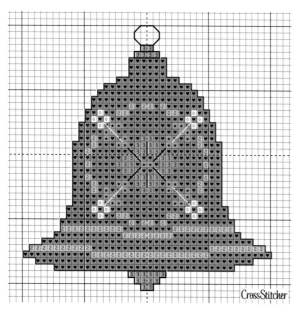

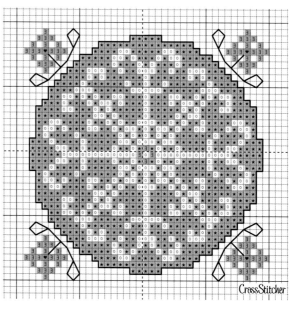

**Cross Stitched Cards for the Holidays**

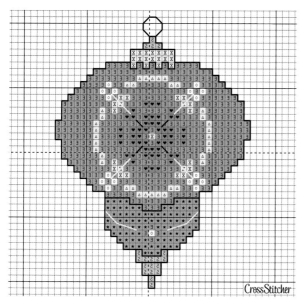

## Make a...
## 3D card

### Step 1

**FOLD** your pale green card in half to create a square card. Cut out a 3 ¾x3 ¾in (9.5x9.5cm) piece of plain white card and attach it to the front of your pale green card using double-sided tape.

### Step 2

**CUT** out your stitching, leaving at least one aida block of space beyond the stitched edge, all the way around. Attach to the center of your card using a few more strips of double-sided tape.

| | DMC | Anchor | Madeira |
|---|---|---|---|
| **Cross stitch in two strands** | | | |
| 0 | B5200 | 001 | 2401 |
| △ | 605 | 1094 | 0613 |
| ∃ | 606 | 334 | 0209 |
| ♥ | 815 | 044 | 0513 |
| ∽ | 956 | 040 | 0611 |
| X | 966 | 240 | 1209 |
| ★ | 3850 | 189 | 1203 |
| **Backstitch in one strand** | | | |
| —— | B5200 | 001 | 2401 |
| dove, tree, present, bell, bauble, angel | | | |

| | DMC | Anchor | Madeira |
|---|---|---|---|
| **Backstitch in one strand** | | | |
| —— | 606 | 334 | 0209 |
| dove, star, tree, present, bauble, angel | | | |
| —— | 815 | 044 | 0513 |
| all other details | | | |
| —— | 956 | 040 | 0611 |
| angel wings | | | |
| —— | 3850 | 189 | 1203 |
| dove, tree | | | |
| **French knots in one strand** | | | |
| ● | 815 | 044 | 0513 |
| angel, dove | | | |

**Switch to aida!** You can always stitch them onto pieces of 14 count white aida instead

There's no trick to stitching on perforated paper. Stitch just as you would on 14 count aida, skipping the hoop of course!

# Traditional Cheer

Stitch Joan Elliott's stylish cards and add some sparkle to your Christmas sentiments!

**Designed by:** Joan Elliott
**Stitch time:** 8 hours

## Materials

- 14 count dark teal aida
- Linen gloss silver cards with an aperture cut to 3x4 ½in (7.3x11.3cm)

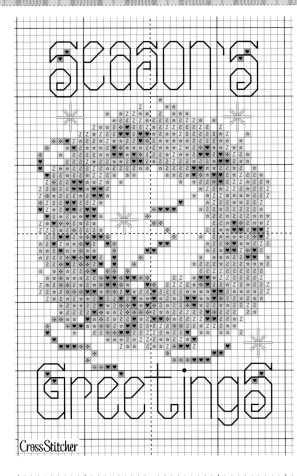

| DMC | Anchor | Madeira |
|---|---|---|
| **Cross stitch in four strands** | | |

★ Madeira Metallic no 4, 4002  *363*

ⓢ Madeira Metallic no 4, 4007  *291*

ⓩ Madeira Metallic no 4, 4010  *pale yellow*

| DMC | Anchor | Madeira |
|---|---|---|
| **Cross stitch in three strands** | | |

♥ 666 046 *red* 0210

✚ 3705 035 *892* 0410

**Backstitch in one strand**

— Madeira Metallic no 4, 4007  *291*
lettering, dove

— Madeira Metallic no 4, 4010  *gold*
dove

| DMC | Anchor | Madeira |
|---|---|---|
| **French knots in one strand** | | |

● 666 046 *red* 0210
dove eye

● Madeira Metallic no 4, 4007  *black*
lettering

**Smyrna stitch in one strand**

✻ Madeira Metallic no 4, 4010  *gold*
stars

Having trouble finding the suggested gold metallic thread? A good alternative is Kreinik Blending Filament 202HL in Aztec Gold.

## DARK COLORED FABRIC

When stitching on dark fabric it's usually a good idea to stitch with three strands of cotton. This will ensure your thread color stands out from the background.

# Little angels

Andrée Langhorn's sparkling Christmas cards are perfect for little angels

Designed by: Andrée Langhorn Stitch time: 8 hours

To make patch cards, simply trim any excess fabric, fray two outer rows all the way around and back with white paper before attaching to the front of your card!

## Materials

- 14 count white aida, 8x6in (20x15cm) each
- Ivory card to fit 4x2¾in (10x7cm) stitched area
- White paper to back your stitching

| Anchor | DMC | Madeira |
|---|---|---|
| **Cross stitch in two strands** | | |
| ✕ 001 | B5200 | 2401 |
| Ǝ 185 | 959 | 1112 |
| ◨ 203 | 954 | 1211 |
| ⌐ 275 | 746 | 0101 |
| O 361 | 738 | 2013 |
| ● 362 | 437 | 2012 |
| ★ 891 | 676 | 2208 |
| ◆ 892 | 225 | 0808 |
| △ 926 | 712 | 1908 |
| · 1009 | 3770 | 2314 |
| ~ 1012 | 754 | 0305 |
| ♡ 1021 | 761 | 0404 |
| ∫ 1092 | 964 | 1104 |
| ∗ DMC Light Effects E3852 | | |
| **Backstitch in one strand** | | |
| —— 400 | 317 | 1714 |
| all other details | | |
| —— 1023 | 3712 | 0405 |
| fairy mouth | | |
| —— DMC Light Effects E3852 | | |
| beaded stars | | |
| **French knots in one strand** | | |
| ● 400 | 317 | 1714 |
| fairy eyes | | |
| **Attach beads with cotton** | | |
| ◉ Mill Hill beads 00557 | | |
| beaded stars | | |

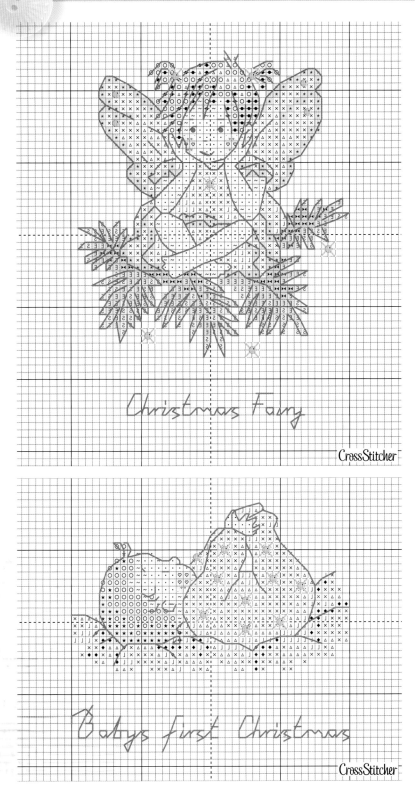

Christmas Fairy

CrossStitcher

Baby's first Christmas

CrossStitcher

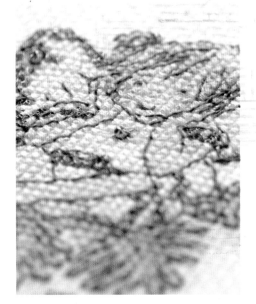

*For super skinny French knots try using a beading needle. They're narrow and long, which is perfect for creating tiny French knots!*

# Let it Snow

These gorgeous snow globes make attractive alternative Christmas cards that your kids will love

**Designed by:** Diane Machin

**Stitch time:** 8 hours

## Card template

Use this template to create your snowglobe base. We chose blue felt, though grey or green would also work well. Attach your felt base to your card using double-sided tape

CrossStitcher

Sarah

Rona

| | DMC | Anchor | Madeira |
|---|---|---|---|
| **Cross stitch in three strands** | | | |
| ✕ | White | 002 *white* | 2402 |
| I | Ecru | 387 *3770* | 2404 |
| ◼ | 310 | 403 *black* | 2400 |
| ◿ | 334 | 977 *930* | 1003 |
| ⌐ | 415 | 398 *light grey* | 1802 |
| Ⴈ | 563 | 208 *472* | 1207 |
| ✛ | 597 | 1064 *959* | 1110 |
| K | 598 | 1062 *BET green* | 1111 |
| S | 704 | 256 *334* | 1308 |
| X | 722 | 323 *363* | 0307 |
| ~ | 828 | 9159 *762* | 1014 |
| Z | 3841 *410* | 159 | 1001 |
| ◨ | 3842 | 164 *royal blue* | 1011 |
| ∩ | DMC Light Effects *3033* E5200 | | |
| **Long stitch in two strands** | | | |
| ▬ | 414 *granite or black* | 235 | 1801 |
| all other details | | | |
| **Backstitch in one strand** | | | |
| ▬ | 414 *granite or black* | 235 | 1801 |
| snow outlines | | | |

CrossStitcher

CrossStitcher

## Materials
- 14 count white aida
- White cards with circular apertures measuring 3¾in (9.5cm) (diameter)
- Blue felt scraps

# Back to basics

This year, wrap your presents with these lovingly handmade rustic tags made with brown card and baker's twine

**Designed by:** Angela Poole
**Stitch time:** 1–2 hours each

| | DMC | Anchor | Madeira |
|---|---|---|---|
| **Cross stitch in two strands** | | | |
| ★ | 469 | 268 | 1503 |
| ◆ | 611 | 898 | 2107 |
| △ | 733 | 280 | 1611 |
| ♡ | 3801 | 1098 | 0411 |
| **Backstitch in one strand** | | | |
| — (leaves and stems) | 469 | 268 | 1503 |
| — (all other details) | 611 | 898 | 2107 |
| **French knots in one strand** | | | |
| ● (eye, star) | 611 | 898 | 2107 |

*Make a…*

## gift tag

*Step 1*

**ONCE** you've finished stitching your design, simply cut some tags out of brown card and trim your aida to fit on the front.

*Step 2*

**ATTACH** your stitched patch to the tag using double-sided tape. Finish by punching a hole in the top for baker's twine.

**Stitch it on rustic!**
For a more earthy finish, try stitching onto 14 count rustic aida instead

# Winter wonderland

We've got your Christmas cards covered with this chic selection of traditional and contemporary designs. Just pick your favorites, grab your threads and get stitching!

**Project by:** Angela Poole and Sharon Blackman
**Stitch Time:** 8 Hours

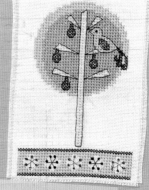

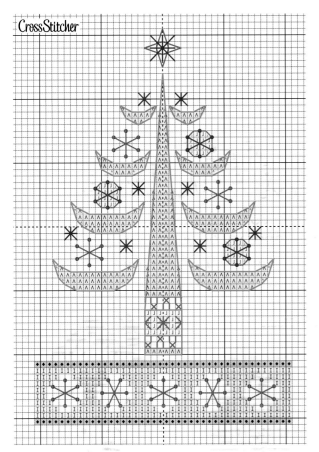

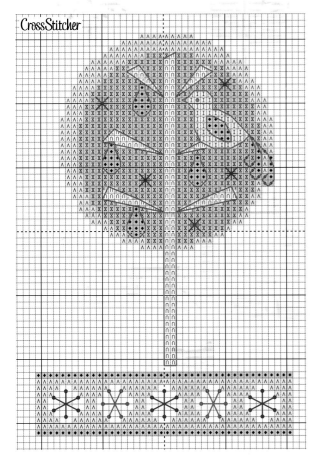

## CRISP FINISH

Back your stitching with a piece of plain white paper before attaching it to the card. This stops the color of the card showing through the holes in your fabric.

## Materials

- 28 count white evenweave, 6¾x8in (17x20cm) for each
- Colored card, 5½x8in (14x20cm), folded in half for each card
- White paper to back your designs

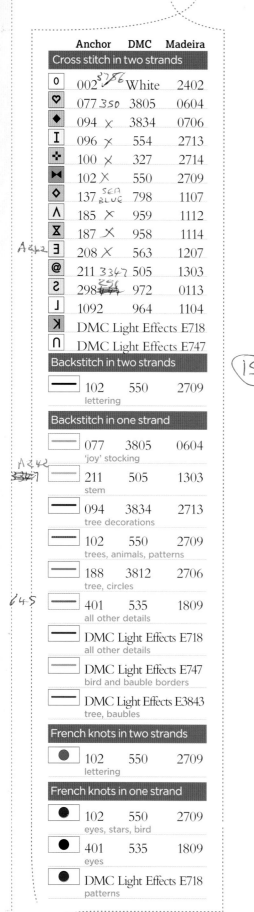

| | Anchor | DMC | Madeira |
|---|---|---|---|
| **Cross stitch in two strands** | | | |
| O | 002 ³⁷⁸⁶ | White | 2402 |
| ♥ | 077 350 | 3805 | 0604 |
| ◆ | 094 X | 3834 | 0706 |
| I | 096 X | 554 | 2713 |
| ✣ | 100 X | 327 | 2714 |
| ◨ | 102 X | 550 | 2709 |
| ◈ | 137 SEA BLUE | 798 | 1107 |
| Λ | 185 X | 959 | 1112 |
| X | 187 X | 958 | 1114 |
| E | 208 X | 563 | 1207 |
| @ | 211 3347 | 505 | 1303 |
| S | 298 | 972 | 0113 |
| L | 1092 | 964 | 1104 |
| K | DMC Light Effects E718 | | |
| U | DMC Light Effects E747 | | |
| **Backstitch in two strands** | | | |
| — | 102 | 550 | 2709 |
| lettering | | | |
| **Backstitch in one strand** | | | |
| — | 077 | 3805 | 0604 |
| 'joy' stocking | | | |
| — | 211 | 505 | 1303 |
| stem | | | |
| — | 094 | 3834 | 2713 |
| tree decorations | | | |
| — | 102 | 550 | 2709 |
| trees, animals, patterns | | | |
| — | 188 | 3812 | 2706 |
| tree, circles | | | |
| — | 401 | 535 | 1809 |
| all other details | | | |
| — | DMC Light Effects E718 | | |
| all other details | | | |
| — | DMC Light Effects E747 | | |
| bird and bauble borders | | | |
| — | DMC Light Effects E3843 | | |
| tree, baubles | | | |
| **French knots in two strands** | | | |
| ● | 102 | 550 | 2709 |
| lettering | | | |
| **French knots in one strand** | | | |
| ● | 102 | 550 | 2709 |
| eyes, stars, bird | | | |
| ● | 401 | 535 | 1809 |
| eyes | | | |
| ● | DMC Light Effects E718 | | |
| patterns | | | |

# Merry Christmas

Send season's greetings across the miles
with these cheerful cards from Maria Diaz

**Project by:** Maria Diaz **Stitch time:** 6 hours each

*Use some adhesive tape to remove any fluff or
fibers from your fabric. It's a great way to keep
your fabric looking clean and fresh!*

## Materials
- 14 count glittery white aida
- Square red cards with an
  aperture of 4x4in (10x10cm)

| DMC | Anchor | Madeira |
|---|---|---|
| **Cross stitch in two strands** | | |
| ✕ White | 002 | 2402 |
| V 156 | 118 | 0902 |
| ⋈ 304 | 019 | 0511 |
| ◪ 317 | 400 | 1714 |
| ♡ 350 | 011 | 0213 |
| ■ 413 | 236 | 1713 |
| ⩽ 436 | 363 | 2011 |
| ∩ 437 | 362 | 2012 |
| ✢ 518 | 1039 | 1106 |
| D 553 | 098 | 0712 |
| ♥ 666 | 046 | 0210 |
| ▲ 700 | 228 | 1304 |
| △ 702 | 226 | 1306 |
| ⦻ 743 | 302 | 0113 |
| ~ 762 | 234 | 1804 |
| I 950 | 4146 | 2309 |
| Z 3755 | 140 | 1013 |
| J 3841 | 9159 | 1001 |
| ★ DMC Light Effects E3852 | | |
| **Backstitch in one strand** | | |
| —— 413 all other details | 236 | 1713 |
| —— 666 bows, lettering | 046 | 0210 |
| —— 700 lettering | 228 | 1304 |
| ----- DMC Light Effects E3852 bow, globe string | | |
| **French knots in one strand** | | |
| ● 413 snowman | 236 | 1713 |
| ● 666 snowman, wreath | 046 | 0210 |

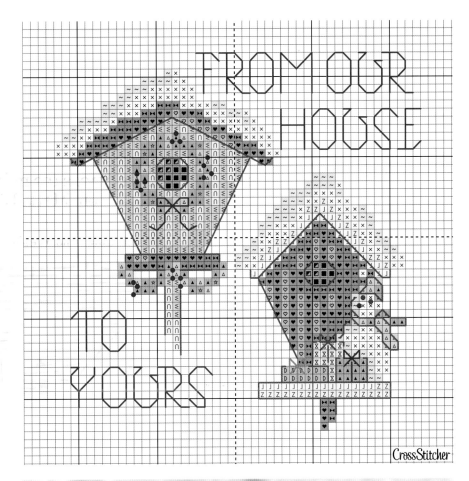

FROM OUR HOUSE TO YOURS

| | DMC | Anchor | Madeira |
|---|---|---|---|
| **Cross stitch in two strands** | | | |
| ✕ | White | 002 | 2402 |
| V | 156 | 118 | 0902 |
| ▶◀ | 304 | 019 | 0511 |
| ◪ | 317 | 400 | 1714 |
| ♡ | 350 | 011 | 0213 |
| ■ | 413 | 236 | 1713 |
| ≤ | 436 | 363 | 2011 |
| ∩ | 437 | 362 | 2012 |
| ✛ | 518 | 1039 | 1106 |
| D | 553 | 098 | 0712 |
| ♥ | 666 | 046 | 0210 |
| ▲ | 700 | 228 | 1304 |
| △ | 702 | 226 | 1306 |
| ⊠ | 743 | 302 | 0113 |
| ~ | 762 | 234 | 1804 |
| I | 950 | 4146 | 2309 |
| Z | 3755 | 140 | 1013 |
| J | 3841 | 9159 | 1001 |
| ★ | DMC Light Effects E3852 | | |
| **Backstitch in one strand** | | | |
| —— | 413 | 236 | 1713 |
| all other details | | | |
| —— | 666 | 046 | 0210 |
| bows, lettering | | | |
| —— | 700 | 228 | 1304 |
| lettering | | | |
| ═══ | DMC Light Effects E3852 | | |
| bow, globe string | | | |
| **French knots in one strand** | | | |
| ● | 413 | 236 | 1713 |
| snowman | | | |
| ● | 666 | 046 | 0210 |
| snowman, wreath | | | |

# A cool yule

Bring some funky style to Christmas this year with these retro designs which use metallic threads for extra sparkle!

**Designed by:** Maria Diaz
**Stitch time:** 8 hours

## Materials

- 14 count white aida, 8x8in (20x20cm) each
- Square white cards with an aperture cut to 4x4in (10x10cm)

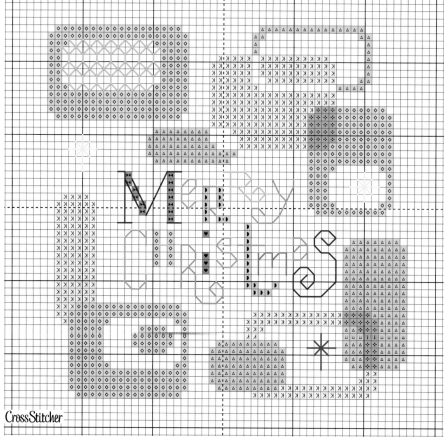

| DMC | Anchor | Madeira |
|---|---|---|
| **Cross stitch in two strands** | | |
| 155 | 109 | 0803 |
| 304 | 1006 | 0509 |
| 351 | 011 | 0214 |
| 704 | 256 | 1308 |
| 958 | 187 | 1114 |
| 964 | 1092 | 1112 |
| DMC Light Effects E815 | | |
| DMC Light Effects E3821 | | |
| DMC Light Effects E3849 | | |
| **Algerian eyes in one strand** | | |
| 351 | 011 | 0214 |
| stars | | |
| 958 | 187 | 1114 |
| baubles | | |
| DMC Light Effects E815 | | |
| stars | | |
| DMC Light Effects E967 | | |
| bauble | | |
| DMC Light Effects E3821 | | |
| stars, baubles | | |
| DMC Light Effects E3849 | | |
| stars, baubles | | |
| **Backstitch in one strand** | | |
| 155 | 109 | 0803 |
| lettering | | |
| 304 | 1006 | 0509 |
| lettering, bauble string | | |
| 351 | 011 | 0214 |
| lettering | | |
| 704 | 256 | 1308 |
| lettering | | |
| 958 | 187 | 1114 |
| bows, lettering | | |
| DMC Light Effects E703 | | |
| bows, bauble string | | |
| DMC Light Effects E815 | | |
| all other details | | |
| DMC Light Effects E967 | | |
| bauble | | |
| DMC Light Effects E3849 | | |
| baubles | | |
| **French knots in one strand** | | |
| DMC Light Effects E815 | | |
| antlers | | |

WHOLE STITCHES ONLY

Cross Stitcher

## METALLIC THREADS

Strengthen metallic threads with a conditioner such as Thread Heaven before you begin. You'll find it stops the threads from fraying as much and will glide through your fabric much easier, too!

## *Mount an…* aperture card

### Step 1

**PLACE** your card face down and stick strips of double-sided tape closely around the aperture edge. Trim the edges of your fabric to fit the aperture.

### Step 2

**PLACE** your stitching face up and turn the card over to position underneath. Keep the fabric grain square to the card edge for an even more professional finish.

### Step 3

**SMOOTH** out fabric creases and press down firmly. Place double-sided tape on the edge of the left-hand panel. For colored cards add a piece of white paper.

### Step 4

**FOLD** the left panel over to line up with the central panel. Press down firmly to flatten the card, fold the third side over and your card is complete!

# Snow place like home

Stitch Brenda Keyes' simple snow-topped
Christmas house for classic homespun appeal

**Designed by:** Brenda Keyes **Stitch time:** 5 hours each

*Give your cards an extra special touch
by adding a ribbon to the top left hand corner.
Tie your ribbon in a bow, cut the ends diagonally
and attach using craft glue—easy!*

## Materials

- 14 count red and navy blue aida, 7x8½in (18x22cm) for each
- Thin ribbon for bows
- White rectangular cards with aperture of 4¾x3¼in (12x8cm)

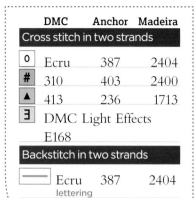

| | DMC | Anchor | Madeira |
|---|---|---|---|
| **Cross stitch in two strands** | | | |
| O | Ecru | 387 | 2404 |
| # | 310 | 403 | 2400 |
| ▲ | 413 | 236 | 1713 |
| Ǝ | DMC Light Effects E168 | | |
| **Backstitch in two strands** | | | |
| ——— | Ecru _lettering_ | 387 | 2404 |

## 14 OR 16 COUNT?

We stitched the snow houses on 14 count aida but you could easily swap that for 16 count instead. Using a smaller count will create a finer look and the design will turn out slightly smaller—perfect if you want a more delicate effect. You don't need to make any changes to the chart—just start stitching on your preferred fabric choice!

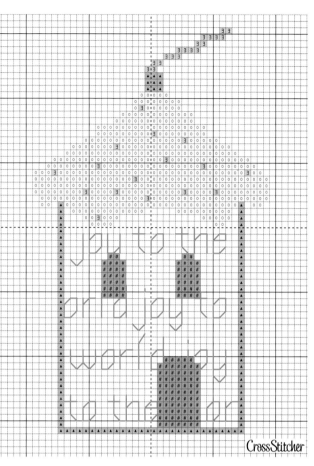

# Festive fairies

Stitch these dainty little sprites and send
some Christmas magic to your loved ones

**Project by:** Andrée Langhorn
**Stitch time:** 7 hours

## Materials

- 16 count antique white aida,
  8x8in (20x20cm)
- Pink aperture cards

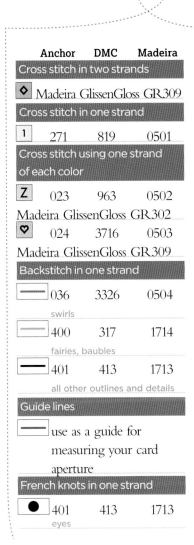

| Anchor | DMC | Madeira |
|---|---|---|
| **Cross stitch in two strands** | | |
| ◇ Madeira GlissenGloss GR309 | | |
| **Cross stitch in one strand** | | |
| 1    271 | 819 | 0501 |
| **Cross stitch using one strand of each color** | | |
| Z    023 | 963 | 0502 |
| Madeira GlissenGloss GR302 | | |
| ♡    024 | 3716 | 0503 |
| Madeira GlissenGloss GR309 | | |
| **Backstitch in one strand** | | |
| ——— 036 | 3326 | 0504 |
| *swirls* | | |
| ——— 400 | 317 | 1714 |
| *fairies, baubles* | | |
| ——— 401 | 413 | 1713 |
| *all other outlines and details* | | |
| **Guide lines** | | |
| ——— use as a guide for measuring your card aperture | | |
| **French knots in one strand** | | |
| ● 401 | 413 | 1713 |
| *eyes* | | |

*For extra sparkle, why not add a few glitzy seed beads?*

CHRISTMAS MAGIC

CHRISTMAS WISHES

# Rainbow brights!

These cartoon Christmas cards will answer
the prayers of busy stitchers and children alike. They're so
quick and easy—perfect for little stitching fingers!

**Project by:** Angela Poole
**Stitch time:** 2–3 hours each

Use a black pen and colored
pencils to add sketchy details
such as the reindeer antlers, but
remember, it doesn't have to be
perfect—just copy ours!

## Top tip!

Perforated paper is a cinch to stitch on, but you can always choose trusty 14 count white aida instead if you like. Just back with iron-on interfacing before cutting out to keep the aida edges from fraying.

| | DMC | Anchor | Madeira |
|---|---|---|---|
| **Cross stitch in two strands** | | | |
| ✕ | White | 002 | 2402 |
| ◗ | 155 | 109 | 0803 |
| ■ | 310 | 403 | 2400 |
| ⊙ | 317 | 400 | 1714 |
| ✕ | 726 | 295 | 0109 |
| I | 746 | 275 | 0101 |
| Z | 747 | 158 | 1104 |
| V | 907 | 255 | 1410 |
| S | 948 | 1011 | 0306 |
| ~ | 963 | 023 | 0503 |
| 9 | 972 | 298 | 0107 |
| 7 | 3078 | 292 | 0102 |
| ♥ | 3607 | 087 | 0708 |
| ∧ | 3608 | 086 | 0709 |
| ♡ | 3609 | 085 | 0710 |
| ⌐ | 3756 | 1037 | 2504 |
| ◪ | 3799 | 236 | 1713 |
| ✛ | 3846 | 1090 | 1105 |
| ⪦ | 3863 | 379 | 1912 |
| Ǝ | 3864 | 376 | 1910 |
| **Backstitch in one strand** | | | |
| — | 155 *bauble* | 109 | 0803 |
| — | 310 *all other details* | 403 | 2400 |
| — | 3607 *bauble* | 087 | 0708 |
| — | 3799 *glove* | 236 | 1713 |
| — | 3846 *bauble* | 1090 | 1105 |
| **French knots in one strand** | | | |
| ● | 310 *eyes* | 403 | 2400 |

## EMBELLISH IT!

You can add as much glitter, buttons and sequins to these cards as you like. Get out your stash, spread out all over the dining room table, and make a big mess. The kids will love it, but secretly you know you will too!

## Materials

- 14 count white perforated paper
- Colored card
- 3D foam pads for mounting
- Black pen and colored pencils
- Sequins, beads and buttons

# Rocking around

The fun doesn't stop when you finish stitching—
this is a Christmas card you can play with too!

**Designed by: Kerry Morgan**
**Stitch time: 11 hours**

## Materials

- 14 count perforated paper, 7x7in (18x18cm)
- Printed or patterned paper, 5¾x6¾in (14.5x17cm)
- White cardstock, 5¾x6¾in (14.5x17cm)

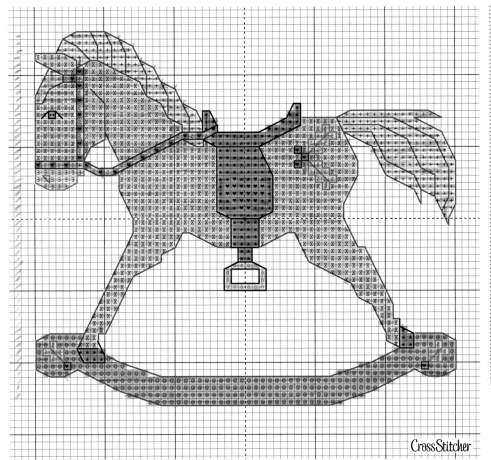

| | DMC | Anchor | Madeira | |
|---|---|---|---|---|
| **Cross stitch in two strands** | | | | |
| 0 | 168 | 234 | 1001 | LIGHT GREY |
| ⋈ | 310 | 403 | 2400 | BLACK |
| ★ | 433 | 358 | 2008 | 393 |
| @ | 435 | 365 | 2010 | 3064 |
| X | 437 | 362 | 2012 | VANILLA |
| 5 | 703 | 238 | 1307 | 1 |
| + | 744 | 301 | 0112 | NATURAL |
| Ǝ | 818 | 023 | 0502 | 2 |
| ♥ | 3801 | 1098 | 0411 | 3 |
| **Backstitch in one strand** | | | | |
| — | 310 | 403 | 2400 | BLACK |
| | eye, saddle, hooves | | | |
| — | 435 | 365 | 2010 | 4 |
| | all other details | | | |
| — | 701 | 227 | 1305 | 5 |
| | holly | | | |
| — | 817 | 013 | 0211 | 816 |
| | berries | | | |
| — | 3706 | 033 | 0409 | 6 |
| | mouth, nose | | | |

CrossStitcher

## Card template

Fold a piece of paper in half and trace this template so the straight edge is in line with the fold, then cut out.

## Make a... rocking card

### Step 1

**BACK** patterned paper with a piece of white card to give it weight and cut out. Alternatively, use the half circle template to create a card from the patterned paper or card of your choice. **CAREFULLY** cut out your horse,

### Step 2

making sure to leave at least one block of space beyond the stitched edges. Embroidery scissors will work best. Attach the bottom half of your horse to the card using double-sided tape.

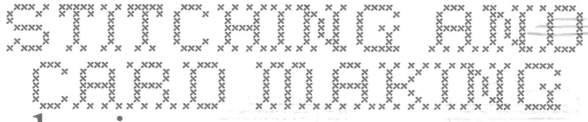

# STITCHING AND CARD MAKING
## basics

## TOOLS OF THE TRADE

### NEEDLES

For basic stitching you'll need a tapestry needle that has a blunt tip and large eye. Use a size 24 needle for most aidas, and a size 26 for evenweaves and linens. Use a sharp embroidery needle for finer details such as backstitch and French knots.

### STRANDED COTTON

Embroidery thread is also commonly referred to as stranded cotton. Each thread length is made up of six strands of cotton twisted together. The chart key will indicate how many strands you'll need to stitch your design with.

### AIDA

Aida is an ideal choice for cross stitch beginners. 14 count is the most common, although it's available in a huge variety of colors and counts. Each cross stitch is worked over a single aida block, making counting and keeping your place a cinch.

### EMBROIDERY SCISSORS

Embroidery scissors are an absolute must-have for stitchers and can be picked up for just a few pounds. Keep yours sharp by only using them to cut threads – that way a decent pair should last you a lifetime.

### HOOPS AND FRAMES

Though not absolutely essential, we do recommend using an embroidery hoop or frame to keep an even stitching tension. Just make sure it's big enough to fit your entire design.

### EVENWEAVE

Evenweave is much simpler to work with than you might think. Start with a 25 or 28 count evenweave, such as Zweigart Lugana. Once you're confident, try your hand at a linen version.

## Make a... simple gift tag

### Step 1

**FOR** super-quick handmade tags, look in local card and stationery shops for ready-made tags to attach your stitching to. Alternatively, dig out your scissors and some brown card and make your own tags. It's really simple and quick to do!

### Step 2

**YOU'LL** need to measure your stitching before you begin to make sure the tag you create is large enough. Draw your tag shape onto paper to use as a template. Trace onto brown or colored card and cut out to create your gift tags.

### Step 3

**FOR** a more crafty finish, try using corner punches and scalloped edge punches to give your tag a different shape. Just make sure you leave enough space at the top to punch a hole for the string. You'll find a single hole punch easiest to use for this part.

### Step 4

**BACK** your finished stitching with white card to stop the tag from showing through the fabric. Then adhere it to the front of your tag using double sided tape. For a 3D finish, mount using a few foam pads instead. Hang with string or bakers twine to finish!

## Make a... quick aperture card

### Step 1

**PLACE** your card face down on the table and stick narrow strips of double-sided tape closely around the aperture edge. Trim the edges of your fabric to fit the card.

### Step 2

**PLACE** your stitching face up and turn the card over to position on the fabric. To keep it straight, match up the grain of your fabric with the edge of the card aperture.

### Step 3

**SMOOTH** out creases and press down firmly. Place double-sided tape on the edge of the left panel. For colored cards add white paper behind the stitching.

### Step 4

**FOLD** the left panel over so it lines up with the central panel. Press down firmly to flatten the card, then fold the third side over the flap and secure to finish.